THE ULTIMATE
GALVESTON
DIET COOKBOOK
FOR BEGINNERS

Lose Weight, Reduce Inflammation, and Prevent Insulin Resistance

SHERRI TODD

GOURMET AND DELICIOUS

INTRODUCTION

Welcome to **"The Ultimate Galveston Diet Cookbook for Beginners,"** a guide designed not only to nourish your body but also to transform your lifestyle. The Galveston Diet is more than just a meal plan—it's a holistic approach to health and well-being that empowers you to take control of your nutrition and live your best life.

Galveston Diet Overview

The Galveston Diet, developed by Dr. Mary Claire Haver, is rooted in the principles of anti-inflammatory eating and intermittent fasting. This diet prioritizes whole, nutrient-dense foods and encourages a balanced intake of healthy fats, lean proteins, and complex carbohydrates. Unlike fad diets that promise quick fixes, the Galveston Diet is a sustainable lifestyle change aimed at achieving long-term health benefits.

Benefits of the Galveston Diet

Adopting the Galveston Diet offers numerous benefits beyond mere weight loss. Followers often experience increased energy levels, improved mental clarity, and a significant reduction in inflammation. These outcomes are not just anecdotal; they are backed by scientific evidence. The diet's focus on anti-inflammatory foods helps to alleviate chronic pain and support overall body health, making it a viable option for those seeking a balanced and evidence-based approach to nutrition.

Reasons to Choose the Galveston Diet

Why choose the Galveston Diet over other dietary approaches? Its simplicity and effectiveness stand out. The diet's emphasis on whole foods makes it easy to follow, even for those new to healthy eating. Unlike restrictive diets that can be challenging to maintain, the Galveston Diet is designed to be a practical and enjoyable part of everyday life. Its focus on nutrient-dense ingredients ensures you receive the vitamins and minerals your body needs without feeling deprived.

What Readers Will Find Inside

This cookbook is your gateway to mastering the Galveston Diet. Inside, you'll discover a diverse array of 50 recipes, meticulously crafted to align with the diet's principles. From 14 hearty breakfast options to kickstart your day, to 14 satisfying lunch recipes that keep you energized, and 14 delectable dinner dishes perfect for unwinding after a long day, every meal is covered. Additionally, we have included 4 delightful snacks and 4 indulgent dessert recipes to satisfy your cravings while staying true to the diet.

Each recipe is designed to be both delicious and easy to prepare, making healthy eating accessible for everyone, whether you're a novice cook or a seasoned chef. You'll find that eating well doesn't mean sacrificing flavor or spending hours in the kitchen.

Additional Information

Beyond the recipes, this cookbook offers insights into the Galveston Diet's core principles and tips for integrating its practices into your daily routine. Whether you're seeking to lose weight, enhance your energy levels, or simply adopt a healthier lifestyle, this cookbook provides the tools and knowledge you need to succeed.

Discover how the Galveston Diet can transform your life. With **"The Ultimate Galveston Diet Cookbook for Beginners,"** you are not just making meals; you are creating a foundation for a healthier, more vibrant you. Enjoy the journey to wellness and savor every bite along the way.

TABLE OF CONTENTS

BREAKFAST RECIPES

BLUEBERRY & SPINACH COLLAGEN SMOOTHIE

Nutrition Information

Calories: 185 kcal   Fat: 5 g
Protein: 7 g   Carbs: 30 g

Ingredients

- 1.5 cups of blueberries
- 1 cup of baby spinach
- ¾ cup of almond milk
- A scoop of collagen
- Ice cubes
- 1 tbsp of almond butter

Directions

1. Wash berries and spinach and pat dry them.
2. Put almond milk, spinach, blueberries, collagen, and almond butter in a blender.
3. Blend on a high speed for a minute.
4. Now add ice cubes and blend for another 30 seconds until a cool, smooth mixture is formed.
5. It is ready to serve.

Prep time
5 Min

Cook time
5 Min

Servings
2

SPINACH AND EGG SCRAMBLE

Nutrition Information
Calories: 303 kcal   Fat: 25 g
Protein: 16 g   Carbs: 4 g

Ingredients
- 2 large eggs
- 1 cup baby spinach
- 1 tbsp olive oil
- Salt & pepper to taste
- 2 tbsp shredded cheese

Directions
1. Wash, pat dry, and chop the spinach.
2. Break and put the eggs in a bowl and sprinkle salt, pepper, and cheese.
3. Beat them well and heat the oil in a pan over medium heat.
4. Add spinach and reduce the heat to a low flame.
5. Cook until the spinach begins to wilt.
6. Pour the egg mixture into the pan over medium heat.
7. Let it set for a bit and then back and forth it with a spatula.
8. It will scramble the egg.
9. Cook until it is set as per your liking.
10. It is ready to serve.

Prep time
5 Min

Cook time
10 Min

Servings
1

GREEK YOGURT BERRY SMOOTHIE

Nutrition Information
Calories: 392 kcal Fat: 10 g
Protein: 25 g   Carbs: 57 g

Ingredients
- ½ cup Greek yogurt
- ½ cup coconut milk
- 1 cup blueberries
- ½ cup strawberries
- 1 tbsp of honey
- Ice cubes

Directions
1. Wash the blueberries and strawberries.
2. Put milk, yogurt, berries, and honey in a blender.
3. Mix them well on a high speed for a minute.
4. Now add ice cubes and blend it for 30 seconds.
5. Pour it into a glass and serve.

Prep time
5 Min

Cook time
5 Min

Servings
2

CHICKEN ROMAINE SALAD WITH AVOCADO

Nutrition Information

Calories: 267 kcal   Fat: 21 g
Protein: 12 g   Carbs: 11 g

Ingredients

Salad

- One chicken breast cut into small cubes
- 1 cup Romaine lettuce
- ½ avocado
- ¼ cups of cherry tomatoes
- 1 tbsp chopped onion
- 1 tbsp olive oil
- Salt and pepper to taste
- 1/1 tsp garlic powder
- ½ tsp onion powder
- 1 tsp lime juice

Dressing

- 1 tbsp lime juice
- 2 tbsp olive oil
- 1 clove minced garlic
- ¼ tsp salt
- ¼ tsp black pepper

Directions

1. Wah, pat dry, and chop the romaine lettuce.
2. Cut avocado into thin slices and half the cherry tomatoes.
3. Marinate the chicken with the spices including salt, pepper, onion powder, garlic powder, and lime juice.
4. Heat the oil on a medium flame and pour chicken in it.
5. Cook for about 2 minutes and flip the sides.
6. Now cook this side for another two minutes.
7. Remove the chicken from the pan.
8. In a small bowl, mix all the dressing ingredients.
9. Put the salad ingredients and chicken in a large bowl.
10. Drizzle the dressing over it and serve.

Prep time
10 Min

Cook time
15 Min

Servings
2

BLT SALMON SANDWICH

Nutrition Information
Calories: 549 kcal   Fat: 43 g
Protein: 12 g   Carbs: 30 g

Ingredients

For Sandwich
- 2 buns
- 4 slices of bacon
- 2 salmon filets
- 2 romaine lettuce leaves
- ½ sliced tomato
- 1 tbsp olive oil
- Salt and pepper to taste

Mayonnaise Spread
- ½ cup mayonnaise
- 1 tbsp chopped herbs
- 1 minced garlic
- Salt and pepper to taste
- ¼ tsp chili powder
- ¼ tsp cumin powder

Directions
1. Wash and pat dry the salmon filets.
2. Heat the olive oil in a pan over medium heat and season the salmon with salt and pepper.
3. Put it in the pan, skin side down, and cook them for 3 minutes.
4. Flip the filets and cook for another 3 minutes.
5. Cook bacon over a medium heat until crispy.
6. Heat the buns over the skillet.
7. Now, mix the spread ingredients in a small bowl.
8. Apply the spread over the bun.
9. Place lettuce, salmon, tomato, and bacon over it.
10. Apply spread over the second half.
11. Make the second bun in the same way and serve.

Prep time
10 Min

Cook time
20 Min

Servings
2

AVOCADO CHICKEN STIR FRY

Nutrition Information

Calories: 494 kcal   Fat: 37 g
Protein: 33 g   Carbs: 37 g

Ingredients

- 2 chicken breasts cut into cubes
- 1 avocado cut into small pieces
- ½ cup chicken broth
- ¼ cup soy sauce
- ½ chopped bell pepper
- ½ cup chopped green onions
- 1 tbsp cornstarch
- 2 tbsp olive oil
- Salt and pepper to taste
- 1 tsp cumin
- 1 minced garlic clove

Directions

1. In a small bowl, mix together chicken broth, soy sauce, cornstarch, and minced garlic.
2. Heat olive oil on medium heat and stir-fry the chicken by reducing the heat a bit.
3. Fry for 5 minutes with continuous stirring.
4. Now add bell peppers, sprinkle salt, pepper and cumin, and fry for another 3 minutes.
5. Now add sauce and green onion.
6. Bring it to a boil and simmer until the desired consistency.
7. It is ready to serve.

Prep time
10 Min

Cook time
20 Min

Servings
2

BREAKFAST

ROASTED CAULIFLOWER WITH TURKEY

Nutrition Information
Calories: 289 kcal   Fat: 17 g
Protein: 26 g   Carbs: 9 g

Ingredients

Turkey
- 1 turkey breast
- 1 tsp brown sugar
- ½ tsp mustard powder
- 1 tsp onion powder
- 1 tsp salt
- 1 tbsp paprika powder

Cauliflower
- 1 head cauliflower
- ¼ cup olive oil
- 1 tsp garlic powder
- 1 tsp onion powder
- 1 tbsp chopped rosemary
- 1 tbsp chopped thyme
- ½ tsp salt
- ½ black pepper
- 1 tbsp oregano

Directions
1. Preheat the oven to 350°F.
2. Cut the stems and leaves of cauliflower.
3. Wash, pat dry, and place it on a greased baking sheet.
4. Mix all the spices for cauliflower in a small bowl.
5. Brush this oil mixture all over the cauliflower and roast it for about 45 minutes or until tender.
6. Now, mix all the turkey spices and rub on both sides of the turkey breast.
7. Cook it in the preheated oven for 1 or 1.5 hours.
8. Serve by placing both in a single dish.

Prep time
15 Min

Cook time
2 Hour

Servings
2

BREAKFAST

GARLIC BUTTER SHRIMP AND BROCCOLI

Nutrition Information
Calories: 230 kcal Fat: 7 g
Protein: 26 g   Carbs: 15 g

Ingredients
- ½ cup broccoli florets
- 350 g shrimp
- 1 tbsp minced garlic
- 2 tbsp of butter
- Salt and pepper to taste
- 1 tsp chili flakes
- 1 tsp paprika powder
- 2 tbsp olive oil

Directions
1. Wash, peel, and pat dry shrimp.
2. Add 1 tbsp of olive oil in a heated pan and cook broccoli for about 6-7 minutes.
3. When it is soft, remove it from the pan.
4. Now add the remaining olive oil and cook the shrimp for about 3 minutes.
5. Flip the sides and cook for another 2 minutes.
6. Remove them from the pan.
7. Add butter and mix all the spices in it.
8. Cook them for a minute, and add shrimp with broccoli.
9. Simmer them for 3 minutes and serve.

Prep time
5 Min

Cook time
20 Min

Servings
2

BREAKFAST

TUNA STEAK

Nutrition Information
Calories: 189 kcal   Fat: 13 g
Protein: 15 g   Carbs: 2 g

Ingredients
- 4 tuna steaks
- 1 tbsp olive oil
- 1 tsp salt
- ½ tsp black pepper
- 1 tbsp minced garlic
- 1 tbsp chopped parsley
- 1 tbsp chopped cilantro
- ¼ cup soy sauce
- ¼ cup water
- 2 tbsp lime juice
- ½ tsp cumin
- 1 tsp paprika powder

Directions
1. Wash and pat dry the tuna steaks.
2. Mix all the spices and pour in a plastic bag.
3. Marinate tuna steaks in it for about 30 minutes.
4. Don't forget to place the bag with steaks in the refrigerator.
5. Heat the olive oil in a grilled pan and cook the steaks for 7-8 minutes for each side.
6. These are ready to serve.

Prep time
30 Min

Cook time
10 Min

Servings
4

BREAKFAST

ROASTED PLUMS WITH GREEK YOGURT

Nutrition Information

Calories: 140 kcal   Fat: 6.4 g
Protein: 3.7 g   Carbs: 6 g

Ingredients

- 2 ripe plums
- 4 tbsp Greek yogurt
- 1 tbsp of honey
- 1 tbsp walnuts
- 1 tbsp brown sugar
- 1 tbsp melted unsalted butter
- 1 tsp cinnamon powder

Directions

1. Wash and cut the plums into halves.
2. Mix half the honey, brown sugar, and cinnamon.
3. Brush the butter on a baking sheet.
4. Preheat the oven to 400 degree fahrenheit
5. Place the plums on the baking sheet and cut side up.
6. Apply the sugar and honey mixture to these plums.
7. Cook them in the preheated oven for about 20 minutes until soft and juicy.
8. Remove from the oven and let them cool.
9. Now add 1 tbsp yogurt to each plum, sprinkle walnuts, and drizzle honey over them.
10. These are ready to serve.

Prep time
10 Min

Cook time
25 Min

Servings
2

BEEF STUFFED MUSHROOMS

Nutrition Information
Calories: 247 kcal   Fat: 19 g
Protein: 4 g   Carbs: 6 g

Ingredients
- 1 cup ground beef
- 5 mushrooms
- ½ cup tomato sauce
- ½ cup water
- Salt and pepper to taste
- 5 tbsp olive oil
- 1 tbsp paprika powder
- ½ cup Mozzarella cheese cubes
- ¼ cup grated Parmesan cheese
- ¼ cup green bell pepper slices
- ½ cup chopped white onions
- 2 tbsp chopped parsley
- 1 tsp minced garlic
- 1 tsp ginger powder

Directions
1. Preheat the oven to 356°F
2. Wash the mushrooms, pat dry them, and remove the stalks.
3. Place the parchment paper on the baking dish.
4. Heat olive oil in a nonstick pan over medium heat.
5. Saute the onions over low-medium heat until soft.
6. Now add green bell pepper and minced garlic to it.
7. Cook for about a minute, and then add ground beef.
8. Sprinkle salt and pepper and cook for about 1 minute.
9. Now add paprika powder, mix well, and cook for another 10 minutes. Put tomato sauce and mix it well.
10. Now add water and ginger powder to it.
11. Mix them well and cook until the water evaporates.
12. Now place the mushrooms on the baking sheet and drizzle some olive oil over them.
13. Fill up the mushrooms with the cooked ground beef.
14. Place 2-3 cubes of Mozzarella on each mushroom and sprinkle Parmesan over them. Drizzle olive oil again over them.
15. Now, bake in the preheated oven for about 20 minutes.
16. Delicious beef stuffed mushrooms are ready to serve.

Prep time
10 Min

Cook time
40 Min

Servings
3

BREAKFAST

BEET SALAD WITH FETA & DILL

Nutrition Information
Calories: 43 kcal   Fat: 5 g
Protein: 0.04 g   Carbs: 1 g

Ingredients
- 1 cup roasted beet cubes
- 1 tbsp olive oil
- 1 tbsp lime juice
- ¼ cup crumbled feta cheese
- 1 tbsp chopped dill
- ¼ tsp black pepper
- ¼ tsp salt

Directions
1. Mix olive oil, lime juice, salt and pepper in a small bowl.
2. Place the roasted beetroots on a serving plate.
3. Drizzle lime dressing over it.
4. Sprinkle feta cheese and dill.
5. The salad is ready to serve.

Prep time
5 Min

Cook time
5 Min

Servings
1

CRISPY TOFU BROCCOLI STIR FRY

Nutrition Information
Calories: 539 kcal   Fat: 13 g
Protein: 26 g   Carbs: 84 kcal

Ingredients
- 1 block tofu
- 3 tbsp olive oil
- Salt and pepper to taste
- 2 cups of broccoli florets
- 2 tbsp olive oil
- 1 tsp ginger garlic paste
- ¼ cup chopped green onions
- Salt and pepper to taste
- ¼ cup low-sodium soy sauce
- ¼ cup vegetable broth
- 2 tbsp balsamic vinegar
- 1 tsp chili flakes

Directions
1. Mix together the soy sauce, broth, vinegar, and chili flakes in a small bowl.
2. Cut the tofu block into 3-inch cubes.
3. Heat 3 tbsp olive oil over a low to medium flame.
4. Sprinkle salt and pepper over tofu cubes.
5. Place them in the pan and cook until golden brown.
6. Make sure to flip the sides every two minutes.
7. Remove them from the pan and heat 2 tbsp olive oil.
8. Add the ginger garlic paste and saute on low heat for 30 seconds.
9. Add broccoli florets and cook for a minute or two.
10. Now add the sauce and cook for two minutes on a high flame until the sauce thickens.
11. Mix tofu in it and pour it onto the serving plate.
12. Sprinkle green onions and serve.

Prep time
5 Min

Cook time
15 Min

Servings
3

RASPBERRY-BEET HUMMUS

Nutrition Information

Calories: 80 kcal   Fat: 6 g
Protein: 3 g   Carbs: 6 g

Ingredients

- 3 red beets
- 1 cup raspberries
- 1 cup cooked chickpeas
- ½ cup olive oil
- Salt and pepper to taste
- 2 garlic cloves
- Juice of one lime

Directions

1. Season the beets with olive oil, salt and pepper.
2. Place them on a cooking sheet with garlic cloves and roast for about 30 minutes at 400˚F.
3. Let them cool and pour in the blender.
4. Now add chickpeas, berries, garlic, lime juice, salt and pepper in the blender.
5. Blend them until a smooth mixture is formed.
6. It is ready to serve.

Prep time
10 Min

Cook time
40 Min

Servings
2

LUNCH
LUNCH

SALMON WITH ASPARAGUS

Nutrition Information

Calories: 29 kcal   Fat: 12 g
Protein: 29 g   Carbs: 18 g

Ingredients

- 4 salmon filets
- 400 g asparagus
- ½ cup olive oil
- 1 tbsp lime juice
- 1 tbsp dried thyme
- 1 tbsp dried parsley
- 3 minced garlic cloves
- ½ tsp salt
- ¼ tsp black pepper

Directions

1. Preheat the oven to 450°F and pat dry the filets and asparagus after washing.
2. Cut the ends of asparagus.
3. Mix all the other ingredients to make a marinade.
4. Place the filets and asparagus on a baking sheet and coat them evenly with the marinade.
5. Bake them for about 13 minutes until it is completely cooked.
6. The salmon is ready to serve by garnishing with chopped parsley.

Prep time
10 Min

Cook time
15 Min

Servings
4

LUNCH

VEGETABLE CURRY STEW

Nutrition Information
Calories: 27 kcal   Fat: 14 g
Protein: 9 g   Carbs: 30 g

Ingredients
- 3 potatoes
- 2 cups of drained and rinsed chickpeas
- 2 cups of carrots
- 2 diced red bell peppers
- 1 can of coconut milk
- ½ cup chicken broth
- 1 chopped onion
- 1.5 tsp salt
- ¼ tbsp black pepper
- 1 tsp curry powder
- 1 tsp brown sugar
- 1 tsp minced garlic
- 1 tsp grated ginger
- ½ tsp cumin powder
- 3 tbsp of olive oil

Directions
1. Peel and cut the potatoes into small pieces.
2. Cut the carrots and potatoes lengthwise.
3. In a cooking pot, heat the olive oil and saute onion for five minutes over low to medium heat.
4. Now add ginger and garlic to cook for another minute.
5. Now, toss the salt, pepper, curry powder, brown sugar, and cumin powder.
6. Cook for 30 seconds, then add broth to it.
7. After this, add the remaining vegetables and sprinkle salt over them.
8. Mix them well and simmer for 50-60 minutes on a low flame. Don't forget to stir occasionally.
9. After this, add the coconut milk and simmer for another minute. Serve immediately.

Prep time
15 Min

Cook time
60 Min

Servings
3

LUNCH

GRILLED CHICKEN SALAD

Nutrition Information
Calories: 480 kcal   Fat: 23 g
Protein: 23 g   Carbs: 12 g

Ingredients
- 2 chicken breasts cut into strips
- 4 cups romaine lettuce
- 1 sliced onion
- 1 chopped avocado
- ½ cup cherry tomatoes cut into halves
- 1 cup sweet corn
- ¼ cup pesto
- Olive oil
- 2 tbsp lime juice
- 1 tbsp Dijon mustard
- ½ cup olive oil
- 2 tbsp honey
- Salt and pepper to taste

Directions
1. Preheat the oven to 400 degrees Fahrenheit.
2. Apply the pesto and a pinch of salt over the chicken pieces to marinate them.
3. Now, heat the grill pan and spray olive oil on it.
4. Cook the chicken pieces for about 4 minutes over low to medium heat.
5. Flip the sides and cook for another 5 minutes.
6. Remove the chicken from the pan and fry corn for about 10 minutes until softened.
7. Mix lime juice, olive oil, Dijon mustard, honey, salt, and pepper to make the dressing.
8. Place romaine lettuce in a large bowl and drizzle half of the dressing over it.
9. Now add vegetables and chicken to it.
10. Drizzle the remaining dressing and serve.

Prep time
5 Min

Cook time
15 Min

Servings
3

LUNCH

GUACAMOLE

Nutrition Information
Calories: 184 kcal   Fat: 16 g
Protein: 3 g   Carbs: 12 g

Ingredients
- 4 ripen avocado
- 2 diced tomatoes
- 1 diced jalapeno
- ¼ cup chopped onion
- ½ tsp salt
- 2 lime juice

Directions
1. Peel and mash the avocado in a large bowl to make a smooth mixture.
2. Now add the remaining ingredients and mix them well.
3. Your Guacamole is ready to serve.

Prep time
5 Min

Cook time
5 Min

Servings
2

ALMOND CHICKEN WITH BROCCOLI

Nutrition Information

Calories: 356 kcal   Fat: 11 g
Protein: 28 g   Carbs: 40 g

Ingredients

- 2 chicken breasts
- 2 cups of broccoli florets

For Marination

- ½ cup almond butter
- 1 tsp fish sauce
- 2 lime juice
- 1 tsp minced garlic
- ½ cup chopped cilantro
- 1 can of coconut milk
- Chili flakes as per your taste
- ½ tsp salt
- 1 tbsp sambal oelek

Directions

1. Mix all the marination ingredients in a bowl.
2. Wash the chicken breasts and cut into small cubes.
3. Add the marination in a large bowl and marinate the chicken with it.
4. Keep it in the refrigerator for an hour.
5. Meanwhile, heat the pan and fry the broccoli florets with some water splashes.
6. Remove them from the pan and add chicken to it.
7. Cook it for 7-8 minutes until the chicken is soft and tender.
8. Make sure to stir in between cooking.
9. Now mix the broccoli in it and serve.

Prep time
10 Min

Cook time
1 Hr 15 Min

Servings
2

LUNCH

COCONUT FISH CURRY

Nutrition Information

Calories: 308 kcal Fat: 20 g
Protein: 26 g   Carbs: 7 g

Ingredients

- 4 cod fish filets cut into half
- 1 can of coconut milk
- 1 cup sliced bell pepper
- 1.5 tsp curry powder
- 2 tbsp olive oil
- ¼ cup sliced onion
- 1 tsp minced garlic
- 1 tsp grated ginger
- Salt and pepper to taste
- ¼ cup chopped fresh cilantro

Directions

1. Heat olive oil in a pan over low to medium heat and saute bell peppers and onions in it.
2. Now sprinkle curry powder and cook for a minute.
3. Now add minced garlic and ginger and sprinkle salt and pepper over them.
4. Cook them for 30 seconds and put fish in them.
5. Add coconut milk and let it simmer for 15 minutes or until the fish is softened.
6. It is ready to serve.

Prep time
5 Min

Cook time
20 Min

Servings
2

LUNCH

THAI PEANUT CHICKEN

Nutrition Information
Calories: 720 kcal   Fat: 35 g
Protein: 86 g   Carbs: 16 g

Ingredients
- 2 chicken breasts cut into strips
- 1 cup broccoli florets
- 1 tsp minced garlic
- 1 sliced onion
- ½ cup peanut butter
- 1 tbsp soy sauce
- ¾ cup chicken broth
- 1 cup coconut milk
- ¼ tsp cayenne powder
- Salt to taste
- 2 tbsp olive oil
- ¼ cup chopped cilantro

Directions
1. Heat olive oil over low to medium heat and cook chicken for about 2 minutes.
2. Remove from the pan and saute onion and florets for 3 minutes on a low flame.
3. Add ginger and garlic and cook for another minute.
4. Now, sprinkle salt and cayenne powder and stir for a minute.
5. Pour peanut butter, coconut milk, and chicken broth into it.
6. Bring it to a boil and add chicken to it.
7. Simmer on a low heat for 10 minutes.
8. Now add soy sauce and simmer for another 2 minutes until thickened.
9. Garnish with cilantro and serve.

Prep time
5 Min

Cook time
20 Min

Servings
2

LUNCH

ZUCCHINI NOODLES WITH PESTO AND SHRIMP

Nutrition Information
Calories: 297 kcal   Fat: 12 g
Protein: 39 g   Carbs: 12 g

Ingredients
- 1 cup zucchini noodles
- 400 g shrimps
- Salt and pepper to taste
- 3 tbsp olive oil
- 1 tsp garlic powder
- ½ tsp paprika powder
- 1 tsp Italian seasoning
- 1 cup pesto sauce

Directions
1. Heat olive oil in a pan and season the shrimp with the spices.
2. Cook them for 2 minutes on low to medium heat until golden brown.
3. Flip the sides and cook for another 2 minutes.
4. Remove from the pan and heat the remaining oil.
5. Add zucchini noodles and let them cook for 3 minutes.
6. Now add shrimp and pesto sauce.
7. Mix them well and serve on a plate.

Prep time
5 Min

Cook time
7 Min

Servings
2

LUNCH

EGGPLANT PIZZA

Nutrition Information

Calories: 331 kcal   Fat: 19 g
Protein: 17 g   Carbs: 25 g

Ingredients

- 2 eggplants
- 1 cup marinara sauce
- 1 cup shredded Mozzarella cheese
- 1 tsp salt
- 1 tsp black pepper
- ¼ cup olive oil

Directions

1. Preheat the oven to 400°F and cut the eggplants into thin round slices.
2. Spread them on the baking sheet and brush olive oil over them.
3. Sprinkle some salt and pepper.
4. Now bake them for 10 minutes.
5. Turn the sides and brush olive oil over them.
6. Bake for another 10 minutes until soft and tender.
7. Now add marinara sauce and top with Mozzarella cheese.
8. Bake them for another 5 minutes until the cheese melts.
9. Eggplant pizza is ready to serve.

Prep time
10 Min

Cook time
25 Min

Servings
4

LUNCH

STUFFED BELL PEPPERS WITH GROUND BEEF AND QUINOA

Nutrition Information

Calories: 362 kcal   Fat: 18 g
Protein: 17 g   Carbs: 36 g

Ingredients

- 4 green bell peppers
- 2 cups chicken broth
- 1 cup quinoa
- 1 cup ground beef
- ¼ cup diced onion
- 1 tsp minced garlic
- ½ tsp oregano
- 2 tbsp tomato sauce
- ¼ tsp salt
- ¼ tsp black pepper
- 1 tbsp olive oil

Directions

1. Preheat the oven to 350 degrees Fahrenheit.
2. Remove the seeds and membranes from the bell peppers to make a space for stuffing
3. Add chicken broth to a saucepan and bring it to a boil.
4. Add quinoa and cook for 20 minutes on a low flame.
5. Meanwhile, heat olive oil in a pan on low to medium heat.
6. Reduce the heat to a low flame and saute onion for about 5 minutes. Now sate garlic for a minute and put ground beef in it. Cook the ground beef until it is browned on a low to medium flame.
7. When quinoa is ready, remove it from the stove.
8. When the ground beef is browned, add salt, pepper, oregano, and tomato sauce to it.
9. Mix them well and cook for a minute.
10. Now add the quinoa in it, mix them well, and cook for another minute.Now, pour the mixture into the bell peppers and place them in a casserole dish.
11. Bake them for 30 minutes and serve.

Prep time
15 Min

Cook time
60 Min

Servings
4

LUNCH

TACO STUFFED SWEET POTATOES

Nutrition Information
Calories: 398 kcal   Fat: 18 g
Protein: 28 g   Carbs: 30 g

Ingredients
- 2 sweet potatoes
- 2 cups of ground beef
- 1 diced onion
- 1 tbsp avocado oil
- ¼ cup chopped lettuce
- 1 tbsp chili powder
- 1 tbsp cumin powder
- ½ tsp garlic powder
- ¾ tbsp salt
- ½ cup shredded Mozzarella cheese
- ¼ cup water

Directions
1. Preheat the oven to 400 degrees Fahrenheit.
2. Poke the sweet potatoes with a fork and bake for 12 minutes.
3. Heat the oil in a pan and saute onions for 3 minutes.
4. Now add the beef and stir for two minutes.
5. Now sprinkle chili powder, salt, garlic powder, and cumin powder.
6. Cook the beef for 5 minutes with continuous stirring.
7. Add water and cook for another 2-3 minutes.
8. Cut the potatoes from the middle lengthwise.
9. Pour the beef and top with the cheese and lettuce.
10. It is ready to serve.

Prep time
10 Min

Cook time
30 Min

Servings
2

LUNCH

CHICKEN AND VEGETABLE SKEWERS

Nutrition Information
Calories: 278 kcal   Fat: 12 g
Protein: 27 g   Carbs: 26 g

Ingredients
- 400 g boneless chicken
- 1 bell pepper cut into cubes
- 1 zucchini cut into small round pieces
- 1 onion cut into cubes
- ¼ cup olive oil
- ¼ cup chopped parsley
- 1 tbsp lime juice
- 1 tsp salt

Directions
1. Mix all the spices except the oil.
2. Marinate chicken and keep it in the refrigerator for an hour.
3. Put the chicken and veggies on the skewers.
4. Heat the oil in a grilling pan and cook it for 10 minutes.
5. Make sure to turn the sides along the way.
6. These are ready to serve.

Prep time
60 Min

Cook time
12 Min

Servings
2

LUNCH

ZUCCHINI AND CARROT FRITTERS

Nutrition Information
Calories: 232 kcal Fat: 22 g
Protein: 5 g   Carbs: 7 g

Ingredients
- 2 large shredded zucchini
- 2 shredded carrots
- ¼ tsp garlic powder
- ¼ tsp black pepper
- ½ tsp salt
- ¼ tsp onion powder
- 1 large egg
- ¼ cup olive oil
- 1 cup almond flour

Directions
1. Remove excess water from the zucchini and carrots.
2. Put them in a large bowl and add all the remaining ingredients.
3. Mix them well and make fritters from them.
4. Heat oil in a pan and cook the fritters for 4 minutes.
5. Flip the sides and cook for another 3 minutes.
6. These are ready to serve.

Prep time
10 Min

Cook time
10 Min

Servings
2

LUNCH

GREEK YOGURT CHICKEN SALAD

Nutrition Information

Calories: 228 kcal   Fat: 6 g
Protein: 27 g   Carbs: 17 g

Ingredients

- 3 cups boneless, cooked and shredded chicken
- 1 cup Greek yogurt
- 1 cup diced celery
- ½ tsp onion powder
- 2 tbsp fresh chopped dill
- 1 tsp salt
- ½ tsp black pepper
- 2 tsp fresh parsley

Directions

1. Take a bowl and add yogurt, parsley, pepper, salt, dill, and onion powder.
2. Mix well until a smooth cream sauce is formed.
3. Now, take another large bowl and put celery, cream sauce, and cooked chicken in it.
4. Combine them well.
5. Sprinkle parsley to serve.

Prep time
5 Min

Cook time
10 Min

Servings
2

LUNCH

DINNER RECIPES

CAULIFLOWER CRUST PIZZA WITH CHICKEN AND VEGGIES

Nutrition Information

Calories: 350 kcal   Fat: 15 g
Protein: 26 g   Carbs: 32 g

Ingredients

- 1 cup cauliflower rice
- ½ cup chicken cut into thin, short strips
- ¼ cup sliced bell peppers
- ½ chopped onion
- 1 egg
- ½ cup shredded Mozzarella cheese
- 2 thinly sliced tomatoes
- 1 tsp minced garlic
- ½ cup spinach
- Salt to taste
- 1 tbsp olive oil

Directions

1. Preheat the oven to 400 degrees Fahrenheit.
2. Mix cauliflower rice, half Mozzarella, egg, garlic, and a pinch of salt.
3. Make a round circle of this mixture on the baking sheet.
4. Bake it for 20 minutes until it makes a crust.
5. Now heat the oil and saute the onion for 5 minutes on a low flame.
6. Add chicken and cook for 5 minutes.
7. Now add bell pepper and spinach to cook until the spinach wilts.
8. Place tomato slices and the mixture on the crust.
9. Now sprinkle the remaining cheese and bake it for 5 minutes or until the cheese melts.
10. It is ready to serve.

Prep time
5 Min

Cook time
40 Min

Servings
1

DINNER

MUSHROOM AND SPINACH STUFFED CHICKEN BREAST

Nutrition Information

Calories: 575 kcal   Fat: 34 g
Protein: 60 g   Carbs: 7 g

Ingredients

- 2 chicken breasts
- 1 cup sliced mushrooms
- 1 cup spinach
- 1 chopped onion
- 1 cup shredded Mozzarella cheese
- Salt and pepper to taste
- 1 tsp minced garlic
- 1 tbsp Italian seasoning
- 4 tbsp olive oil

Directions

1. Cut the chicken breast lengthwise to make pockets for the filling.
2. Heat 1 tbsp olive oil in a pan and saute onion for 3 minutes.
3. Now add minced garlic and cook for 30 seconds.
4. Add mushrooms and cook for 5 minutes.
5. Now, put the spinach and sprinkle Italian seasoning over it.
6. Cook them with continuous stirring until the spinach is wilted.
7. Sprinkle salt and pepper inside and out of the chicken breasts.
8. Fill the pockets with the mushrooms and spinach picture.
9. Top with the cheese and seal the cut with the toothpick.
10. Heat the remaining oil and cook the chicken breasts for 7-8 minutes on low to medium heat from each side.
11. It is ready to serve.

Prep time
10 Min

Cook time
25 Min

Servings
2

DINNER

GREEK STYLE LAMB KEBABS WITH TZATZIKI SAUCE

Nutrition Information
Calories: 373 kcal   Fat: 17 g
Protein: 48 g   Carbs: 6 g

Ingredients

For Lamb Kebabs
- 1 pound lamb cut into small cubes
- 1 tsp oregano
- Salt and pepper to taste
- 1 tsp minced garlic
- 1 tbsp olive oil
- 2 tbsp lime juice

For Sauce
- 2 cups of Greek yogurt
- ½ cup chopped cucumber
- Salt and pepper to taste
- ¼ cup chopped onion
- ¼ cup chopped parsley

Directions
1. Mix all the sauce ingredients in a small bowl.
2. Mix olive oil, lime juice, minced garlic, oregano, salt, and pepper to make the marination.
3. Coat the lamb pieces with this marination and leave it for 2 hours overnight in the refrigerator.
4. Put them on the skewers and heat the grilling pan.
5. Cook them well for two minutes on each side.
6. Serve it with the Tzatziki sauce.

Prep time
10 Min

Cook time
20 Min

DINNER

Servings
4

BAKED COD WITH ROASTED VEGETABLES

Nutrition Information

Calories: 221 kcal Fat: 12 g
Protein: 21 g Carbs: 11 g

Ingredients

- 2 cod filets
- ½ cup carrots cut into round shape
- ¼ cup sliced bell peppers
- ¼ cup sliced onion
- ½ cup cherry tomatoes cut into halves
- Salt and pepper to taste
- ½ tsp garlic powder
- 2 tbsp olive oil

Directions

1. Preheat the oven to 400 degrees Fahrenheit.
2. Place the vegetables on the baking sheet and the cod filets in the middle of them.
3. Drizzle olive oil over them and season with salt, pepper, and garlic powder.
4. Bake them for about 25 minutes.
5. Baked cod with roasted vegetables is ready to serve.

Prep time
10 Min

Cook time
25 Min

Servings
2

DINNER

SHRIMP AND AVOCADO SALAD

Nutrition Information
Calories: 363 kcal Fat: 3 g
Protein: 25 g   Carbs: 12 g

Ingredients
- 1 pound cooked shrimp
- 2 sliced avocados
- 2 cup shredded lettuce leaves
- 1 tbsp lemon juice
- 1 tsp paprika
- 2 tbsp chili sauce
- ⅓cup mayonnaise
- 2 tbsp chopped chives
- Salt to taste

Directions
1. Firstly, take a bowl and put the chives, mayonnaise, chili sauce, and shrimp in it.
2. Mix them well and season with salt.
3. Now, put the avocado slices in the mixture.
4. Drizzle lemon juice on the top.
5. Place the mixture on the lettuce leaves dusted with paprika.
6. The salad is ready to serve.

Prep time
5 Min

Cook time
10 Min

Servings
2

DINNER

TURKEY MEATBALLS WITH MARINARA SAUCE

Nutrition Information

Calories: 347 kcal Fat: 18 g
Protein: 27 g   Carbs: 19 g

Ingredients

- 500 g ground turkey
- 1 tsp minced garlic
- ½ cup chopped onion
- 1 large egg
- 1 tsp salt
- ¼ tsp black pepper
- ½ tsp oregano
- 1 jar marinara sauce
- 2 tbsp olive oil

Directions

1. Remove all the water from the chopped onion.
2. In a large bowl, mix together the turkey, salt, pepper, garlic, oregano, onion, and egg.
3. Make small meatballs from this mixture.
4. Heat the oil over medium heat and cook the meatballs for 8 minutes.
5. Make sure to thoroughly cook each side of the meatballs.
6. Now pour the marinara sauce and simmer for 15 minutes.
7. It is ready to serve.

Prep time
10 Min

Cook time
30 Min

Servings
3

DINNER

GRILLED CHICKEN CAESAR SALAD

Nutrition Information

Calories: 388 kcal   Fat: 14 g
Protein: 41 g   Carbs: 19 g

Ingredients

- 453 grams chicken
- 1 tbsp lemon juice
- 2 minced garlic cloves
- Salt and pepper to taste
- 1 tsp dried thyme
- 2 tbsp olive oil
- 1 tsp lemon juice
- ¼ cup shredded cheese
- Salt and pepper to taste
- 2 tbsp wine vinegar
- ¼ chopped garlic
- 1 tsp anchovy paste
- 2 tsp mustard paste
- ½ cup yogurt
- 2 tbsp parmesan cheese
- 4 slices wheat bread
- 2 halved Romaine lettuce
- Salt and ground pepper

Directions

1. Take a bowl and put yogurt, garlic, anchovy paste, mustard paste, cheese, lemon juice, vinegar, pepper, and salt.
2. Mix all the ingredients well.
3. Cover the mixture and put it in the refrigerator until used.
4. First of all, take a small bowl and mix all the chicken spices to make marination. Season the pepper and salt on the chicken.
5. Pour the marinade mixture on the chicken, put it in a seal and massage the chicken, with your hands. Place it in the refrigerator for an hour.
6. Preheat the grill pan over medium-high heat and brush it with oil.
7. Put the chicken on the grill and cook for 4-6 minutes.
8. Flip and cook for another 4-6 minutes.
9. Remove the chicken from the grill and grill the romaine lettuce and bread.
10. Sprinkle the olive oil on them and season them with salt and pepper.
11. Now, place the cut side romaine lettuce and cook for 2-3 minutes until nicely grilled.
12. Cut the bread into cubes.
13. Place the grilled romaine lettuce cut side on the serving plate and top the grilled bread, chicken, parmesan cheese, Caesar dressing, salt, and pepper.
14. Serve and enjoy.

Prep time
1 Hr 20 Min

Cook time
15 Min

Servings
3

DINNER

BAKED TILAPIA WITH LEMON AND HERBS

Nutrition Information
Calories: 270 kcal   Fat: 14 g
Protein: 34 g   Carbs: 1.2 g

Ingredients
- 2 filets Tilapia fish
- ½ cup chopped parsley
- 1 tbsp lime juice
- ¼ tsp black pepper
- 1 tsp salt
- ½ tsp minced garlic
- ¼ cup olive oil

Directions
1. Wash and pat dry the fish.
2. Preheat the oven to 400 degrees Fahrenheit.
3. In a small bowl, add oil, lime juice, salt, pepper, and parsley.
4. Coat the fish evenly with this mixture.
5. Place the filets on a baking sheet lined with parchment paper.
6. Bake the fish for about 12 minutes.
7. It is ready to serve.

Prep time
5 Min

Cook time
15 Min

Servings
2

DINNER

LEMON HERB ROAST CHICKEN

Nutrition Information
Calories: 405 kcal   Fat: 29 g
Protein: 32 g   Carbs: 4 g

Ingredients
- 1 whole chicken
- 1 tsp salt
- ¼ cup lemon slices
- ½ cup rosemary
- ¼ cup chopped parsley
- 1 tsp oregano
- 1 tsp minced garlic
- ½ tsp minced thyme
- ¼ tsp black pepper
- ½ cup chicken broth
- ¼ cup olive oil

Directions
1. Clean, wash and pat dry the whole chicken.
2. Mix all the remaining ingredients in a small bowl.
3. Preheat the oven to 390 degrees Fahrenheit.
4. Apply half of the mixture inside and half outside of the chicken.
5. In a baking dish, add lemon slices and pour the chicken broth.
6. Place a rack over the dish
7. Put chicken over the rack and bake for 30-40 minutes.
8. It is ready to serve.

Prep time
10 Min

Cook time
40 Min

Servings
4

DINNER

RATATOUILLE WITH QUINOA

Nutrition Information

Calories: 275 kcal Fat: 10 g
Protein: 10 g   Carbs: 43 g

Ingredients

- 1 cup quinoa
- 2 cups of water
- 2 cups of diced eggplants
- ½ cup diced onion
- ½ cup diced bell peppers
- 1 zucchini cut into slices
- ½ cup cherry tomatoes cut into halves
- 2 tbsp olive oil
- ½ tsp black pepper
- 1 tsp salt
- ½ tsp paprika powder
- ½ tsp garlic powder
- ¼ tsp thyme
- ¼ tsp rosemary
- ½ tsp oregano

Directions

1. Preheat the oven to 450 degrees Fahrenheit.
2. Mix all the spices except the olive oil.
3. Prepare two baking sheets and line them with parchment paper.
4. Place onions, bell peppers, and zucchini on one sheet.
5. Place the tomatoes and eggplants on the other sheet.
6. Drizzle half the olive on one sheet and the remaining on the other sheet.
7. Divide herbs in two equal amounts and sprinkle equally on both the sheets. Bake them for 10 minutes, then stir them. Bake for another 10 minutes.
8. Boil water in a saucepan and pour quinoa in it. Cook for 20 minutes and let it cool. Mix the vegetables and quinoa.
9. It is ready to serve.

Prep time
10 Min

Cook time
30 Min

Servings
3

DINNER

BALSAMIC GLAZED PORK TENDERLOIN

Nutrition Information
Calories: 300 kcal   Fat: 9 g
Protein: 40 g   Carbs: 12 g

Ingredients
- One pound pork
- 1 tsp minced garlic
- 1 tbsp olive oil
- Salt and pepper to taste
- ⅓ cup balsamic vinegar
- 2 tbsp brown sugar
- 2 tbsp soy sauce

Directions
1. Mix olive oil, minced garlic, salt, and pepper.
2. Preheat the oven to 375 degrees Fahrenheit.
3. Rub this mixture all over the tenderloin.
4. Bake it for about 15 minutes.
5. In the meantime, vinegar, sugar, and soy sauce in a saucepan.
6. Simmer on a low flame until it thickens.
7. Pour it over the pork and bake for another 15 minutes.
8. Slice the tenderloin and serve.

Prep time
10 Min

Cook time
30 Min

Servings
2

DINNER

TURKEY CHILI WITH BEANS

Nutrition Information

Calories: 211 kcal   Fat: 6 g
Protein: 22 g   Carbs: 16 g

Ingredients

- 907 grams turkey
- 2 cup chopped onions
- 2 tbsp chopped garlic
- 1 tbsp olive oil
- 2 tbsp chili powder
- 1.5 tsp cumin powder
- 1.5 tbsp tomato paste
- 1 can cannellini beans
- Salt and pepper to taste
- 1.5 cup chicken stock
- ½ cup chopped cilantro

Directions

1. Place a large cooking pan with olive oil over medium heat.
2. Saute onion for 3 minutes and add garlic to it.
3. Fry it for half a minute and add turkey.
4. Cook it for 6 minutes with frequent stirring.
5. Now, add the chili powder, cumin, tomato paste, beans, salt, and pepper.
6. Mix them well and add chicken stock to it.
7. Bring it to a boil and lower the heat to simmer for 10 minutes.
8. Sprinkle cilantro and serve.

Prep time
5 Min

Cook time
20 Min

Servings
3

BUTTERNUT SQUASH SOUP

Nutrition Information
Calories: 305 kcal   Fat: 4 g
Protein: 7 g   Carbs: 60 g

Ingredients
- 1360 gram butternut squash
- 2 tbsp olive oil
- 1 large chopped onion
- 3 chopped garlic cloves
- 3 cup vegetable broth
- 1 chopped carrot
- Pepper and salt to taste
- ½ tbsp minced rosemary

Directions
1. Take a cooking pot and heat oil in it over medium flame.
2. Add squash, carrot, and onions and cook for 5 minutes until brown.
3. Now, pour the vegetable broth into the pot and bring it to a boil.
4. After that, cover the pot, stir and cook for 40 minutes until the vegetables are tender.
5. Put the mixture in a blender and blend until smooth.
6. Put it in a bowl and season it with salt and pepper on top.
7. Serve and enjoy.

Prep time
10 Min

Cook time
50 Min

Servings
3

DINNER

STUFFED ACORN SQUASH

Nutrition Information

Calories: 388 kcal   Fat: 18 g
Protein: 13 g   Carbs: 47 g

Ingredients

- 2 halved acorn squash
- 2 tbsp olive oil
- ½ cup chopped onions
- 2 minced garlic cloves
- 226 grams of sliced mushrooms
- 1 tbsp vinegar
- ½ tbsp chopped rosemary
- ¼ cup dried cranberries
- Parsley for garnish
- Ground black pepper and salt to taste
- 226 grams tempeh

Directions

1. First of all, preheat the oven to 425°F and line a baking sheet with parchment paper.Remove the seeds from the squash and put the halves of the squash on the baking sheet.
2. Sprinkle olive oil and a pinch of salt and pepper on the squash halves. Roast its cut side for 40 minutes until tender. Now, cut the tempeh into cubes and place them in a steam basket.
3. Set over the pot with 1-inch deep water in it. Bring it to a simmer and steam for 10 minutes. For crumbling the tempeh, drain out the excess water with your hands.
4. After that, take another cooking pot and heat olive oil in it over medium heat. Add onions and black pepper and cook for 5 minutes. Now, add the mushrooms and cook for 8 minutes with continuous stirring until soft.
5. Add garlic, vinegar, tamari, tempeh, and rosemary and cook for 2-3 minutes. When the pan gets dry, add more water. Put in the cranberries and season with salt and pepper to taste.
6. Spoon this mixture into roasted halved acorn squash and garnish with parsley.
7. Serve and enjoy.

Prep time
15 Min

Cook time
1 Hr 20 Min

Servings
3

DINNER

SNACKS RECIPES

GREEK YOGURT PARFAIT

Nutrition Information

Calories: 298 kcal   Fat: 11 g
Protein: 21 g   Carbs: 28 g

Ingredients

- ½ cup yogurt
- 1 tbsp honey
- 2 tbsp granola
- 2 fresh fruits of your choice

Directions

1. First of all, take a bowl and make a yogurt layer on the bottom.
2. Add half granola, fresh fruits, and honey in it.
3. Make another layer of yogurt over the granola and fruits.
4. Toss some fruits and granola on top.
5. Serve and enjoy.

Prep time
3 Min

Cook time
5 Min

Servings
1

SNACKS

CUCUMBER HUMMUS BITES

Nutrition Information
Calories: 20 kcal   Fat: 1 g
Protein: 1 g   Carbs: 2 g

Ingredients
- 1 sliced cucumber
- 16 cherry tomatoes cut into halves
- Chopped parsley to taste
- 283 grams Hummus
- 56 grams of crumbled feta cheese

Directions
1. Firstly, wash the cucumbers, cut them into round slices and place them on a plate.
2. Spoon the hummus on the top of each slice of cucumber with a teaspoon.
3. Toss parsley, cheese, and cherry tomatoes on the top.
4. Serve and enjoy.

Prep time
5 Min

Cook time
10 Min

Servings
2

SNACKS

AVOCADO DEVILED EGGS

Nutrition Information

Calories: 239 kcal   Fat: 20 g
Protein: 8 g   Carbs: 10 g

Ingredients

- 6 large and boiled eggs
- 1 large diced avocado
- 1 tbsp cilantro
- Salt and pepper to taste
- ¼ tsp garlic powder
- 1 tbsp lime juice

Directions

1. Halve the boiled eggs carefully without cutting the yolk, and place them in a bowl.
2. Add the avocado to the bowl and mash by using a fork until smooth.
3. Now add egg yolks and mashed with avocados.
4. Sprinkle the pepper, salt, and garlic powder and stir until blended.
5. Spoon the mixture into the halved eggs with a spoon, and toss salt and pepper on top.
6. Serve and enjoy.

Prep time
5 Min

Cook time
10 Min

Servings
3

SNACKS

ROASTED CHICKPEAS

Nutrition Information
Calories: 119 kcal   Fat: 1 g
Protein: 5 g   Carbs: 15 g

Ingredients
- 2 cans of cooked chickpeas
- 1 tbsp olive oil
- 2 tbsp paprika powder
- ½ tsp salt
- ¼ tsp black pepper
- 1 tsp garlic powder

Directions
1. Preheat the oven to 425°F.
2. Take a baking sheet lined with parchment paper.
3. Place the cooked chickpeas on a towel, dry them, and remove the loose skin.
4. Place them on the baking sheet and toss olive oil, black pepper, garlic pepper, paprika pepper, and salt over them.
5. Roast chickpeas for 20-30 minutes in the preheat oven until crispy and golden brown.
6. Remove from oven and toss your favorite sauces if you want to
7. Store chickpeas in a container at room temperature.
8. Serve and enjoy.

Prep time
10 Min

Cook time
30 Min

Servings
5

SNACKS

DESSERTS
RECIPES

BAKED APPLES WITH CINNAMON AND WALNUTS

Nutrition Information

Calories: 380 kcal Fat: 19 g
Protein: 4 g   Carbs: 55 g

Ingredients

- 4 apples
- ½ cup chopped walnuts
- 85 grams almonds
- 1 tbsp olive oil
- 2 tbsp ground cinnamon
- Brown sugar to taste

Directions

1. Preheat the oven to 350°F
2. Core all the apples by using a knife or an apple corer and place them on a baking sheet.
3. Take a bowl and add almonds, walnuts, cinnamon, and sugar.
4. Fill all the core apples with the walnut mixture and toss the oil on top of the apples.
5. Bake them in the preheated oven for 34-35 minutes until tender.
6. Remove the apples from the oven and place in a bowl.
7. Serve them and enjoy.

Prep time
10 Min

Cook time
35 Min

Servings
4

DESSERTS

BERRY CHIA SEED PUDDING

Nutrition Information

Calories: 343 kcal   Fat: 15 g
Protein: 14 g   Carbs: 39 g

Ingredients

- ½ cup of strawberries
- ½ cup blueberries
- ½ cup blackberries
- 6 tbsp chia seeds
- 1 cup almond milk
- ½ tsp vanilla extract
- 1 tsp maple syrup
- 1 cup granola

Directions

1. First of all, put the strawberries, blueberries, blackberries and milk in a blender and combine until smooth.
2. Remove the mixture in a bowl, add syrup, chia seeds, and Vanilla extract and mix well.
3. Now, cover the mixture and put it in the refrigerator for 8 hours.
4. Take two bowls and put the mixture in them, toss some barriers on the top, serve and enjoy

Prep time
5 Min

Cook time
10 Min

Servings
2

BAKED PEARS WITH CINNAMON AND GREEK YOGURT

Nutrition Information
Calories: 241 kcal   Fat: 1 g
Protein: 7 g   Carbs: 57 g

Ingredients
- 3 halved pears
- ½ cup yogurt
- ⅓ cup honey
- ½ cup granola
- 1 tbsp ground cinnamon
- 2 tbsp Vanilla extract
- Mint leaves for topping

Directions
1. First of all, preheat the oven to 350°F.
2. Core each pear in half by using a round teaspoon and place them in a baking dish.
3. Now, take a bowl and mix cinnamon, honey, and vanilla.
4. Apply this mixture over the pears.
5. Bake the pears in the preheated oven for 15-18 minutes until tender.
6. Remove them from the oven and toss yogurt and a few teaspoons of granola on top.
7. Serve and enjoy.

Prep time
5 Min

Cook time
20 Min

Servings
3

DESSERTS

GRILLED PINEAPPLE WITH HONEY AND CINNAMON

Nutrition Information

Calories: 130 kcal   Fat: 9 g
Protein: 1 g   Carbs: 31 g

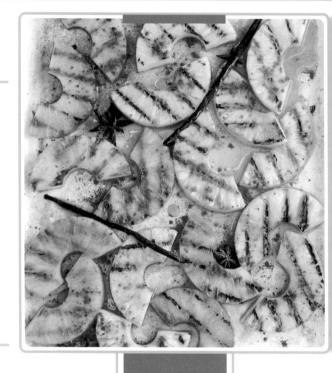

Ingredients

- 1 large pineapple
- 4 tsp brown sugar
- 4 tsp honey
- 1 tsp cinnamon
- 1 tbsp Olive oil

Directions

1. First of all, wash the pineapple and cut it into round-shaped slices.
2. Heat olive oil in a grilling pan.
3. Now, grill all the pineapple slices over medium heat for 5-10 minutes.
4. Remove from heat and toss cinnamon, brown sugar, and honey on top.
5. Serve and enjoy.

Prep time
5 Min

Cook time
10 Min

Servings
56

2 WEEK MEAL PLAN
WEEK 1

Day	Breakfast	Lunch	Dinner	Snack	Dessert
1	Blueberry & Spinach Collagen Smoothie	Salmon With Asparagus	Cauliflower Crust Pizza With Chicken And Veggies	Greek Yogurt Parfait	Baked Apples With Cinnamon And Walnuts
2	Spinach And Egg Scramble	Vegetable Curry Stew	Mushroom And Spinach Stuffed Chicken Breast	Cucumber Hummus Bites	Berry Chia Seed Pudding
3	Greek Yogurt Berry Smoothie	Grilled Chicken Salad	Greek Style Lamb Kebabs With Tzatziki Sauce	Avocado Deviled Eggs	Baked Pears With Cinnamon And Greek Yogurt
4	Chicken Romaine Salad With Avocado	Guacamole	Baked Cod With Roasted Vegetables	Roasted Chickpeas	Grilled Pineapple With Honey And Cinnamon
5	BLT Salmon Sandwich	Almond Chicken With Broccoli	Shrimp And Avocado Salad	Greek Yogurt Parfait	Baked Apples With Cinnamon And Walnuts
6	Avocado Chicken Stir Fry	Coconut Fish Curry	Turkey Meatballs With Marinara Sauce	Cucumber Hummus Bites	Berry Chia Seed Pudding
7	Roasted Cauliflower With Turkey	Thai Peanut Chicken	Grilled Chicken Caesar Salad	Avocado Deviled Eggs	Baked Pears With Cinnamon And Greek Yogurt

2 WEEK MEAL PLAN
WEEK 2

Day	Breakfast	Lunch	Dinner	Snack	Dessert
8	Garlic Butter Shrimp And Broccoli	Zucchini Noodles With Pesto And Shrimp	Baked Tilapia With Lemon And Herbs	Roasted Chickpeas	Grilled Pineapple With Honey And Cinnamon
9	Tuna Steak	Eggplant Pizza	Lemon Herb Roast Chicken	Greek Yogurt Parfait	Baked Apples With Cinnamon And Walnuts
10	Roasted Plums With Greek Yogurt	Stuffed Bell Peppers With Ground Beef And Quinoa	Ratatouille With Quinoa	Cucumber Hummus Bites	Berry Chia Seed Pudding
11	Beef Stuffed Mushrooms	Taco Stuffed Sweet Potatoes	Balsamic Glazed Pork Tenderloin	Avocado Deviled Eggs	Baked Pears With Cinnamon And Greek Yogurt
12	Beet Salad With Feta & Dill	Chicken And Vegetable Skewers	Turkey Chili With Beans	Roasted Chickpeas	Grilled Pineapple With Honey And Cinnamon
13	Crispy Tofu Broccoli Stir Fry	Zucchini And Carrot Fritters	Butternut Squash Soup	Greek Yogurt Parfait	Baked Apples With Cinnamon And Walnuts
14	Raspberry-Beet Hummus	Greek Yogurt Chicken Salad	Stuffed Acorn Squash	Cucumber Hummus Bites	Berry Chia Seed Pudding

Made in the USA
Columbia, SC
16 September 2024

42420378R00035